In Fields of Prairie Fire

Hunter Burr

BookLeaf Publishing

Presentation by *BookLeaf Publishing*

Web: www.bookleafpub.com

E-mail: info@bookleafpub.com

ISBN: 9789357210676

First edition 2022

DEDICATION

To the flowing River.

I'd never have picked up a pen again

if you had not shown me how to hold it.

I dedicate this to you.

Desert Flower

Soak your saliva
into the cracks of dry clay
surrounding my desert heart

And breathe into me, a new spring

Helena

I hold the love of the World
In the palm of my hand

Still, I set it down
to interlock with yours

Cards

I am a homemaker
In this house of cards

Dusting ever so gently
Tidying up with my breath on pause

So as not to wake you
Not to stir you
Not to lose you

Let me stay

A Cherry Underfoot

Touch the small of my back once again…
Trace your initials there, make my skin burn
Brand me like cattle, prod and poke at me with amusement

I'm yours, a thousand ways
This broken body, this graffiti-covered chapel
No grace necessary, crush my cherry underfoot

Use me
Bruise me
Bleach my blushed skin
And dye it red in sugary syrup
Make me more digestible for your eyes
…and touch the small of my back once again

Andromeda

Every touch a petal
Every kiss a star
For you
My andromeda
I have left my heart ajar

Lost to the Sea

The weight of the tides
Pulling my heart
Feel so cumbersome

And the dragging of the East wind
To draw my breath
Feels so forceful

But the weight of living
Without you
Is the only thing I cannot bear

The Morning After Love

This is not I love you
But it is a sweet goodbye

It is the last drag
Before I quit cold-turkey
The final punch
Before I throw in the towel
On the morning after love

It has to be the end
Because it tastes so sweet

The after-notes of sage
In a highball glass of whiskey
The taste of mint chapstick
Caught only the morning after love
On this the morning after love

Hold twice and let go
On this the morning after love
And begin this sweet goodbye

Thanksgiving

Break stale bread in half
At a table of people I do not recognize
And tell me it's thanksgiving

What are we so thankful for?

Frozen Wings

We're brought into this world
Cracked from the sacred egg
Through the great suffering of our own mothers
On a bed of dew-covered flowers

We fly for the first time
Soaking our feathers in the warm summer sun

But just as we've entered, we must make our exit
At the end of the 7th act
Facedown in the snow
Through a great suffering of our own
Our bones crack and cry out
No longer are we in the sacred egg
Only after this
Are we with our mothers once again

Serpent

Hold the decanter
As I bathe in the water which was once wine

I need to cleanse myself
Rinse the taste of exploration from my tongue
And the smell from my hair and neck

I need to forget
Forget the lonely feeling of this island I inhabit
That is just a little too close to the sun
Forget that I am made of wax
Melting under pressure, too afraid of freedom

Allow me the space
To cleanse and repent
Do not be abhorred
As I tell you
The charms of the serpent

I may have bit the apple
But allow me this grace
Keep me in the garden
And let me share this space

No matter how much I beg

This grief has not ceased
I've turned every page of this flawed scripture
Such that a page in revelations has creased

No answers have appeared
And everything is dark
I have lost my faith
The fire within me, its spark

If the lord is a just man
He will guide me through
But until then
I guess I must start anew

The drops hit my tongue in a steady stream
across
This does not taste like wine
As I wipe away the fog from my mirror,
I see the yellow of my eyes
The scales…
And for a moment, I swore I let out a hiss

I grasp at my chest, grasp for the silver to scare
away the serpent
But it is not there
Never was, in fact

I may pray so long for salvation
Until my knees are weak

And my palms grow sweaty in their clasped nature

But it changes nothing
I lured myself from the garden
And make pie from every forbidden apple

I threw away my salvation
Without forethought, without prayer
And this is what I deserve

Lord, please forgive me
For this is what I deserve

Heavy

My heart
It is so heavy
That it lifts and drops like a stone mallet
On my diaphragm
Rhythmic, karmic, torture

I need water
To make it stop
slow the drop
To make it float
Like a lily pad

And I'll be at peace again

Left for Dead at the Dinner Table

Put your knees together
Keep your elbows down
Clasp your small hands on the placemat
Do not move them around

She taught me what was right
How to be a lady
I still remember all the habits
Even though the memories are hazy

Now I sit across the table
Knees together, elbows down
My hands clasp a cocktail
Maintaining composure as best I am able

Your ankle hooks mine underneath the table
Your elbows drape across while you stroke my arm
Up and down, up and down
Oh right, I'm at the table

I must be quiet
I must be still
Keep my voice down to nothing but a trill

Let you feast upon me with your gaze
Lick my skin and bite at it
I'll hold the napkin while you graze

I was never taught how to eat
How to feast
How to fill my belly
Or the belly of the beast

I was raised like lamb for the slaughter
Taught to be hunted
Eaten
Broken
Beaten
Bitten

And left for dead at the dinner table

Beautiful Words

Let us raise a litost
To the image of your happiness
My dear

Clink our glasses in the cacophonous clamber of
nothing more left to discuss

Sit in silence next to me and occupy your
memory as I have
With the reprise of redamancy
Only found in the former frisson of our folly
To fully be free in the arms of the other

Until such a time may come where I can boast a
broader bounty of beautiful words for your
wonder

Make do with the mouthful I can spell with a
split tongue
And a full heart

Hopeful

Maybe one day
I can write you well enough

I can print our memories on every page
And rehearse every verse

I can perform our dances
And sing all our favorite songs

I'll swirl my cochlea like fine wine
Until I drown you out

And then I'll write some more

Deprivation

Mark me with the sign of the times
As the smell of loneliness and desperation floods my nose

In these days of distance
The touch of someone, anyone, is guilt-ridden ecstasy

I sit in the back of a crowded-empty club
And watch the yearning flow

I hear the couple in the booth behind me make a hotel room of this empty space
And I think of you

Please, don't stop
Are you going to help me find that breath I lost?

Maybe I'll find it in between your parted lips
Or better yet I'll steal yours from you

As wave rolls over wave
In a dance in which the tempo matches our need

I find us becoming one form, then two, then one again
Just like that
Just like that

I need you to stop
But please don't stop
I need you to be gentle
As I've been deprived for so long
Oh god
Oh god

Before I know it, they are finished, and I must end my inner prose

When I am home, I sit on my balcony alone
Waiting

I see the woman across the street 2 floors up
Tending to her delicate rose

I watch her needing flow
And think of me

Wrap this hand around our neck
And feel our pulse grow quicker in anticipation

Who do we imagine tonight?

Will it be him again?
Let's just see where our hand guides us

Will we only reach the surface
Circling
Or will we venture
Deeper, Deeper

Stop

A final cry, an arch and a playful whisper into nothing says "I love you" to no one in particular

I imagine our cries meet somewhere in the atmosphere, dancing in the empty space between our wanton hearts

It is here where we can meet in the middle
Where the needing feels needless
And we're all together once again

Yeshua

Watch me as I write this
And guide my trembling hand

As my faith drains from the tip of this quill
Show me the second set of footprints in the sand

Take me to the place
Where the water suddenly becomes land

Walk with me in this place
Please take my outstretched hand

Solstice

Frost
Covering the fall harvest

Patches and groves and orchards and fields
O'er which the wind howls

A scarecrow salutes the morning rise of the sweet, suckling autumn sun

Time to get to work

If

If all I can write is of pain
Of strife
Of life
Of drain
Then as long as you are by my side

I shall never write again

Denim Day

You've come this far
But come no further
You've taken what you will
But I will free no more
From the heart cage of my chest
Abreast
I walk in the summer sun
Parallel to the mountains

You will not take the seasons from me
You will not take the love of my body
For you've come this far
But you will come no further
Unto me

Dried

Dry my heart
In the Tularosa sun

Covered in the white sands of purity and time
Watch how
At once it hardens like ceramic
And forgets how to love them

Finding

I'm remembering how it felt to be a child of the desert
Making bouquets of prairie fire
Feeling the magnetism of the earth pointing me
North between two mountain peaks

The cold fog tickles bare skin of my back
Fresh ink and sage leaves
But the January sun is at my front

I'm searching for the heart of the city
In the middle of the night
In the light of day
A flaneur in the flame
Discovering the way of the urbanite

I'm learning to be happy
I'm learning to be kind
I'm learning to want, but not need
I'm bouncing ideas, making plans
Being here, not leaving it there
I'm making it work
I'm writing it down
Turning the pages
Pages upon pages

Upon pages upon pages
Every day

www.ingramcontent.com/pod-product-compliance
Lightning Source LLC
Chambersburg PA
CBHW051757130826
49812CB00033B/1186